DRUGS IN REAL LIFE

STEROIDS

BY SUE BRADFORD EDWARDS

CONTENT CONSULTANT

NICHOLAS RATAMESS, PHD, CSCS*D, FNSCA
PROFESSOR, DEPARTMENT OF HEALTH AND EXERCISE SCIENCE
THE COLLEGE OF NEW JERSEY

D1212378

Essential Library

An Imprint of Abdo Publishing | abdopublishing.com

ABDOPUBLISHING.COM

Published by Abdo Publishing, a division of ABDO, PO Box 398166, Minneapolis, Minnesota 55439. Copyright © 2019 by Abdo Consulting Group, Inc. International copyrights reserved in all countries. No part of this book may be reproduced in any form without written permission from the publisher. Essential Library™ is a trademark and logo of Abdo Publishing.

Printed in the United States of America, North Mankato, Minnesota
042018
092018

THIS BOOK CONTAINS
RECYCLED MATERIALS

Cover Photo: Shutterstock Images
Interior Photos: Lee Jin-man/AP Images, 5; Hassan Ammar/AP Images, 8; Alexander Zemlianichenko/ AP Images, 12; Shutterstock Images, 14–15, 37, 39; iStockphoto, 18, 43, 44–45, 73; Andreas Gebert/picture-alliance/dpa/AP Images, 21; Dr P. Marazzi/Science Source, 24–25; Doug Kapustin/ The Washington Post/Getty Images, 29; Michael Bryant/Philadelphia Inquirer/MCT/Newscom, 33; Larry Strong/KRT/Newscom, 34–35; Leonard Lessin/Science Source, 48; Blue Ring Media/ Shutterstock Images, 51; Daniel Dash/Shutterstock Images, 53; Smith Collection/Gado/Archive Photos/Getty Images, 55; Paul Sakuma/AP Images, 56–57; Manuel Balce Ceneta/AP Images, 59; Roger L. Wollenberg/UPI Photo/Newscom, 61; Paul Connors/AP Images, 65; Joel Saget/AFP/Getty Images, 66; Denis Kuvaev/Shutterstock Images, 68–69; Jasminko Ibrakovic/Shutterstock Images, 75; Wayne Jones/AP Images, 77; LM Otero/AP Images, 79; Red Line Editorial, 82; Monkey Business Images/Shutterstock Images, 83; Africa Studio/Shutterstock Images, 86; Craig Warga/NY Daily News Archive/Getty Images, 89; Wulf Pfeiffer/picture-alliance/dpa/AP Images, 92–93; Jürg Carstensen/ picture-alliance/dpa/AP Images, 95; Kevin Wolf/AP Images, 98

Editor: Maddie Spalding
Series Designer: Laura Polzin

Library of Congress Control Number: 2017961356

Publisher's Cataloging-in-Publication Data

Names: Edwards, Sue Bradford, author.
Title: Steroids / by Sue Bradford Edwards.
Description: Minneapolis, Minnesota : Abdo Publishing, 2019. | Series: Drugs in real life | Includes online resources and index.
Identifiers: ISBN 9781532114205 (lib.bdg.) | ISBN 9781532154034 (ebook)
Subjects: LCSH: Steroids--Juvenile literature. | Steroid abuse--Juvenile literature. | Athletes--Drug use--Juvenile literature. | Drug control--United States--Juvenile literature.
Classification: DDC 362.29--dc23

CONTENTS

DOPING AT THE OLYMPICS

On the evening of August 7, 2016, the Olympic announcer called the names of the women preparing to swim. As each name was read, supporters and spectators cheered and waved national flags. When the announcer read the name of Yulia Efimova from Russia, her supporters probably cheered and clapped. But no one could hear them over the booing.

When she arrived at Rio de Janeiro, Brazil, for the Summer Olympics, Efimova was the women's world champion in the 100-meter breaststroke. But that wasn't enough to earn her the respect of the crowd. In 2013, she had tested positive for dehydroepiandrosterone (DHEA), a steroid supplement.

Because of this, the International Federation for Swimming (IFS) took away Efimova's world titles and banned her from competition for 16 months. Efimova won the title in the 100-meter breaststroke after the ban, but early in 2016 she tested positive for another drug: meldonium.

Meldonium can be used as a prescription to treat respiratory and lung infections as well as heart disease, but athletes sometimes use it as a performance-enhancing drug (PED). It is not a steroid, but it enables the body to carry more oxygen. This improves the athlete's performance when she exerts herself. Testing positive for this PED could have kept Efimova out of the Olympics. In mid-July, the IFS cleared her of the charges so she could compete in August.

But that wasn't enough to keep spectators from all over the world from booing when her name was called.

At the sound of the horn, the swimmers dove into the pool and powered through the water. Efimova won her preliminary

DHEA

The anabolic-androgenic steroid DHEA is banned by the Olympics, the World Anti-Doping Agency, the National Collegiate Athletic Association (NCAA), the National Football League (NFL), and the National Basketball Association (NBA). Despite this, it is sold in stores throughout the United States because it is not a controlled substance. It is considered a supplement, similar to a vitamin caplet. Most DHEA is made in China from wild yam roots. Supporters say DHEA is safe to use, but there have been no long-term studies of its side effects.

heat and exited the pool, walking past reporters with a smile and one finger raised to signal she was number 1. Spectators again booed. US swimmer Lilly King mockingly waved her finger back at Efimova.

When asked about her gesture, King said she relished competing against top swimmers from around the world at the Olympics. Reporters asked King whether she thought Efimova should have been allowed to compete in the Olympic Games. "It was the IOC's [International Olympic Committee's] decision and I'm going to respect that decision, even though it's not something I agree with," King said.[1]

Some US athletes who competed in the 2016 Olympics had a history of doping as well. Track-and-field sprinter Justin Gatlin had tested positive for anabolic-androgenic steroids (AAS) in 2006. He had been banned from competition for four years. He later competed in the 2016 Olympics and won a silver medal in the 100-meter race. Sprinter Tyson Gay had tested positive for AAS in 2013 and was banned from competition for one year. The IOC stripped Gay and his fellow relay runners of the silver medal they had won in the 2012 London Olympics, but Gay went on to participate in the 2016 Olympics. Asked whether athletes who have been caught doping should be on the US Olympic team, King said, "They shouldn't. It is unfortunate we have to see that."[2]

Steroids are chemical compounds that are naturally produced within the human body. But AAS are synthetic, or

US track-and-field athletes Tyson Gay, *left,* and Justin Gatlin, *second from left,* were forced to give up a silver medal they had won in the 2012 Olympics after Gay tested positive for AAS.

manufactured, steroids. "Anabolic" refers to a synthetic steroid's muscle-building properties. "Androgenic" refers to male sexual characteristics, which AAS users tend to develop. AAS mimic the effect of natural steroids, such as testosterone, by increasing muscle mass and strength. For those reasons, AAS give users an advantage over athletes who do not take AAS.

DOPING SCHEMES

On June 17, 2016, the International Association of Athletics Federations (IAAF) banned the entire Russian track-and-field team from competition in the 2016 Olympics because of a state-run doping scheme. AAS were used to enhance the performance of Russian athletes at the 2008 Olympics in Beijing, China; the 2012 Olympics in London, England; and the 2014 Olympics in Sochi, Russia. Prior to each of these Olympic

Games, Russian doctors had given athletes a blend of three banned drugs, including AAS. Athletes quit taking the mixture a week or two before competition so that the drugs would not show in their urine, but a second plan was also put into place.

Dr. Gregory Rodchenkov, the former director of Russia's national drug-testing laboratory, explained that potentially tainted urine samples from Russian athletes were replaced with clean urine samples prior to the 2014 Olympics. A lab tech would take urine samples from Russian athletes who had been doping and pass the samples through a hidden hole in the lab wall to an accomplice outside the lab. This accomplice would then give the tech within the lab clean urine. The accomplice would destroy the tainted samples. By substituting untainted urine for urine that might reveal the use of banned drugs, Russian athletes passed their urine tests.

The Russian government claimed to be working to make certain that its athletes were

LANCE ARMSTRONG

In 2012, the US Anti-Doping Agency (USADA) released a lengthy report based on eyewitness testimony and financial records. The report condemned US cyclists, including Lance Armstrong. Armstrong had won the elite Tour de France from 1999 to 2005. He also won a bronze medal in cycling at the 2000 Summer Olympics in Sydney, Australia. Although Armstrong had never failed a drug test, when his blood was retested, it showed testosterone levels that were not normal. The IOC demanded Armstrong return his medal. The International Cycling Union also took away his seven Tour de France titles. Armstrong finally admitted he had used PEDs and AAS for much of his career.

Dr. Grigory Rodchenkov estimated that 100 tainted urine samples from Russian athletes were exchanged with clean urine as part of the 2014 Russian Olympic team's doping scheme.[3]

not taking banned substances for the 2016 Olympics. But early in the summer of 2016, British authorities who test athletes for these substances had been threatened by members of Russia's Federal Security Service. These same authorities also said that many Russian athletes had not provided samples for testing in the month before the IAAF voted on the ban.

Although the Russian team could not compete as a whole, individual athletes could participate. To do so, they had to prove that they had not taken part in the doping scheme. They also had to show that they had been out of the country and thus away from the influence of Russian officials, perhaps attending college overseas. In addition, they had to volunteer to be tested for AAS and other banned drugs.

The IOC asked the federations overseeing various sports to verify that Russians competing in their areas had not taken banned substances. Many athletes tested positive for such substances. Others did not meet the criteria set to prove they were outside of the influence of Russian officials. In total, 118 Russian athletes, including weightlifters, rowers, and canoeists, were banned. Only 271 Russian athletes were allowed to compete.[4] The IOC also wanted to catch those who had cheated in earlier games, which meant retesting old samples.

ABUSE OF AAS

AAS are different from drugs such as cocaine, heroin, and opium-based painkillers. People who abuse AAS are not taking them to get high or to dull pain. Using AAS can be rewarding to athletes, but these drugs do not give a person a chemical rush.

People who take AAS want to change how they look or improve their athletic performance. They see these drugs as an easy way to build bigger, stronger muscles, and, through these muscles, confidence or a competitive advantage in sports. They want these results so badly that they do not consider the damage AAS can do.

An athlete who uses AAS has a physical advantage over athletes who do not. Because of this, many sports organizations

TESTING FOR AAS

Urinalysis, or a urine test, is the most common way to test for AAS. These tests look for an abnormal amount of testosterone, or more than is normally present in a person's body. One test compares the level of testosterone to the level of the hormone epitestosterone. A urine test that shows a ratio of four parts or more of testosterone for every one part epitestosterone means the person may be using AAS. An athlete who fails a urine test that examines testosterone levels may then be given another urine test that examines carbon isotopes. This test can tell the difference between endogenous and exogenous steroids. Endogenous steroids are produced by the athlete's body. Exogenous steroids originate outside the athlete's body. A carbon isotope test looks at cholesterol from the athlete's body. The lab compares the weight of the carbon in the cholesterol with the weight of the carbon in the testosterone. If they have similar weights, the testosterone was produced in the athlete's body. If the weights vary significantly, the lab will know the athlete has been taking AAS.

Technicians work at Russia's national drug-testing laboratory in 2016. An investigation by the World Anti-Doping Agency uncovered a doping scheme that had been carried out in this lab.

have banned the use of AAS. The IOC first banned AAS in 1975 when a reliable urine test was developed. It was used to test for AAS at the 1976 Winter Olympics in Montreal, Canada. But professional athletes are not the only people who abuse AAS. Many high school athletes and other teenagers also abuse AAS.

Because AAS are similar to natural hormones, some people think they are safe. AAS are derived from testosterone, a naturally occurring hormone. These testosterone derivatives are chemically similar to testosterone, which allows them to interact with the human body much as testosterone does. Hormones are chemical messengers that act on human cells. Some hormones aid in digestion. Some, such as testosterone, stimulate growth. Other hormones influence metabolism, fertility, or other bodily functions. Another reason some people think AAS are safe is because they can be prescribed by doctors.

AAS can be used to treat certain illnesses and diseases. But AAS use without a prescription can lead to addiction and drug abuse. Drug abuse causes harmful effects on the user's mind and body. It is because of these dangers that AAS are illegal without a prescription. Despite this, many people are willing to risk the dangers because of the benefits they hope to gain by taking AAS.

RETESTING

The IOC can retest samples for up to ten years following a competition. When the doping scheme used by the Russian government came to light, the IOC retested samples from the 2008 Beijing Games and the 2012 London Games. The IOC found 23 new cases of doping in the 265 London samples and 31 new cases in the 454 Beijing samples. The Russian Olympic Committee admitted that nearly half of these new cases involved Russian athletes, 11 of whom were in track and field.[5]

CHAPTER TWO

STEROIDS AND TESTOSTERONE

Testosterone is a hormone produced by the human body. Both men's and women's bodies make testosterone, although men make more. Small quantities of testosterone are produced by the adrenal glands, found above the kidneys, in both men and women. Testosterone is also produced in the ovaries in women and the testes in men. Just how much testosterone someone needs to be healthy depends on the person's age and gender, but both men and women need testosterone for good health. Testosterone contributes to the sex drive, helps in the production of red blood cells, and promotes bone and

Advertisements for steroids often promote their muscle-building potential, which is caused by synthetic testosterone.

muscle growth in both men and women. Both men and women who have low testosterone may have a low blood count, a low sex drive, and problems reproducing.

In males, testosterone levels increase sharply at the beginning of adolescence. Testosterone drives the physical changes associated with puberty. These changes include increased muscle mass and bone density, reduced fat, a deepening voice, and hair growth. These characteristics that emerge during puberty are called secondary sexual characteristics. Because more muscle mass contributes to burning fat calories, increased muscle mass means a more efficient metabolism and less fat. A man's production of testosterone begins to drop once he reaches 30 years old.

When not enough testosterone is produced in a male's body, the result is hypogonadism. An adolescent without enough testosterone may not mature physically or

HORMONALLY SPEAKING

Hormones are chemical messages that travel through the blood to the tissues and organs. It takes only a small amount of a hormone to trigger its function. Some hormones help in the digestion of food and affect mood and behavior. Others, including testosterone and estrogen, help people mature sexually. Estrogens and progestogens, the primary steroids in women, are made in the ovaries. Testosterone is needed for the testes to produce sperm in men, and estrogen is needed for the ovaries to make ova in women. Sperm and ova are needed for reproduction. Hormones are essential to good health, but too much of a hormone can cause as much trouble as too little.

undergo the sudden growth spurt expected at this stage. An adult male who has low testosterone may have no sex drive. He may be unable to achieve and sustain an erection or produce sperm. He may also lose muscle mass and gain weight as his body burns fat less efficiently.

People whose bodies do not produce enough testosterone may be prescribed AAS by their doctor. The AAS might be testosterone, or it might be another androgen. Androgens, produced in the testes and the adrenal glands, are the primary reproductive steroids in men. Testosterone is a type of androgen.

Corticosteroids are also produced by the adrenal glands. Two types of corticosteroids are mineralocorticoids and glucocorticoids. Mineralocorticoids regulate the balance of water, sodium, and potassium in the body. Glucocorticoids enable the breakdown of proteins and also cause glycogen, a form of carbohydrate, to be stored in the liver. One glucocorticoid, called cortisol, is a hormone that affects how people respond to stress.

TESTOSTERONE CONFUSION

The effects of testosterone are highly complex. It is hard to understand exactly what testosterone does because it does not work alone. Some of the testosterone a man's body makes is converted into the hormone estradiol. As a man's body produces less testosterone, it necessarily produces less estradiol. This means that some of the effects blamed on low levels of testosterone may actually be the result of low levels of estradiol.

Cortisone in inhalers helps people with asthma breathe more easily.

Cortisol helps reduce inflammation, or swelling, in the body. It also suppresses allergic reactions, including itching and redness. Cortisone is a synthetic version of cortisol. It provides relief for inflamed or swollen tissue. How it is administered depends on what is being treated. As a gel or cream, it treats itchy bug bites and rashes. It dilates blood vessels in the skin to reduce redness and swelling. As an inhaler, it treats asthma, reducing inflamed tissue in the lungs. Cortisone shots are used to treat arthritis. They are injected into inflamed joints to reduce swelling.

EUREKA

Beginning in the late 1800s, doctors and scientists experimented with using testosterone to relieve the symptoms of hypogonadism and aging. Charles E. Brown-Séquard, a French doctor who studied the function of hormones, reported on an infamous series of experiments in 1889. Brown-Séquard noticed that as he aged, he was less energetic. To counteract this, he injected himself under the skin daily with one milliliter of an experimental mixture he called the Brown-Séquard Elixir. This elixir was made up of testicular vein blood and semen. These liquids came from either a dog or a guinea pig. After 20 days, he noted in his journals that "[a] radical change took place in me. I had regained at least all the strength I possessed a good many years ago."[1]

Scientists now know that this improvement was not from the elixir itself. It was a placebo effect. Because Brown-Séquard expected the elixir to work, he convinced himself that he felt stronger and more energetic.

These types of experiments dropped off after scientists discovered artificial testosterone. This discovery occurred in the 1930s after German chemist Adolf

AAS AND THE PLACEBO EFFECT

In 1972, researchers Gideon Ariel and William Saville studied a group of athletes for 11 weeks. They told 15 weightlifters that whoever progressed the most in lifting weights by midway through the program would be given AAS. Randomly chosen "winners" were given a placebo. No one received real AAS. Before the placebo, they each added an average of 5.8 pounds (2.6 kg) to the weight they could squat. By the end of the study, the athletes given the placebo each added an average of 41.8 pounds (19.0 kg) to the weight they could squat. They improved much more than those who had not received the fake AAS.[2]

Butenandt isolated the human sex hormones testosterone and progesterone. He and another scientist discovered that these hormones could be synthesized, or created in the lab, from androsterone, a type of androgen. During this same period, scientists realized that if they gave laboratory animals exogenous steroids, the animals grew larger muscles faster than was possible without the steroids. This led to experimentation in which human athletes were given AAS.

When the US Olympic weightlifters went to the 1954 World Weightlifting Championships in Vienna, Austria, American physician Dr. John Ziegler was told by a Soviet doctor that the Soviet weightlifters were using testosterone. The US weightlifters lost to the Soviets. When Ziegler got back to the United States, he started experimenting with testosterone.

In 1958, Ziegler worked with the company Ciba Pharmaceuticals to develop the AAS Dianabol. Ziegler and Bob Hoffman gave Dianabol as a pill to weightlifters who trained at York Barbell gym in Pennsylvania. Hoffman managed the gym and also coached Olympic weightlifting. Ziegler and Hoffman wanted to see what effects the drugs would have on weightlifters. The athletes, eager to bulk up, took large

A healthy man normally produces less than 10 milligrams of testosterone daily, but a male athlete looking to bulk up may take more than 100 milligrams of exogenous testosterone per day.[3]

doses of what they called "Doc Ziegler's mysterious pink pills."[4] When combined with physical training, athletes who took these Dianabol pills quickly became more muscular.[5]

Although Ziegler had been instrumental in developing the use of AAS among athletes, he later stopped encouraging athletes to take Dianabol. In time, he realized that many of the athletes who used this AAS developed liver conditions. He said that he regretted giving Dianabol to the athletes.

OVER THE COUNTER

In the 1990s, a few anabolic steroid precursors were sold as over-the-counter supplements in the United States. Over-the-counter supplements can be purchased by anyone. A buyer doesn't need a doctor's prescription to buy them. Anabolic steroid precursors, also called prohormones, are substances that the body can convert into anabolic steroids,

AAS AND LIVER DISEASE

Many AAS, including Dianabol, have been linked to liver disease and liver cancer. To be effective, AAS have to circulate in the bloodstream for as long as possible. The liver's job is to cleanse the blood by filtering out a variety of impurities. Dianabol and other AAS have been engineered so that the molecules are harder for the liver to break down and remove from the blood. This means that the AAS continues to circulate in the bloodstream, putting strain on the liver as it works to remove the AAS. An early sign of liver failure is the yellowing of a person's skin and eyes. This happens as impurities build up in a person's body. If the liver completely ceases to function, the person has only days to live. The good news is that liver damage is reversible if it is caught early enough.

including testosterone. A common prohormone that was sold over the counter as a pill or capsule was androstenedione, or andro.

Prohormones were sold as nutritional supplements for athletes. Nutritional supplements are meant to add or increase certain nutrients in a person's diet. Vitamins, minerals, and sports nutrition products are all common supplements. Certain supplements, such as vitamin C, may help people get the vitamins and minerals they need to be healthy. But because supplements are subject to fewer studies and tests before they are sold to consumers than are pharmaceuticals, the health benefits of supplements can be questionable. Scientists and doctors do not know how effective these supplements are at doing what the manufacturers claim. They also don't know what side effects these supplements may produce or how serious the side effects might be. Without a doctor's advice, people do not have limits or guidance on the supplements they take. Many people take as much of the supplement as they think they will need to give them the results they want.

Prohormones were made illegal in the United States with the Anabolic Steroid Control Act of 2004. This law went into effect in 2005. Research into whether prohormones increased testosterone levels, as their manufacturers claimed, ended when prohormones were made illegal.

THE DOCTOR KNOWS BEST

People take AAS for a variety of reasons. Some abuse AAS because they want to build lean muscle, look thinner, or excel in a sport. Others use them legally as prescriptions to treat various medical conditions or illnesses. Because of this need, they are made by pharmaceutical companies around the world.

MANUFACTURING STEROIDS

In 1927, Fred C. Koch, a professor of physiological chemistry at the University of Chicago, realized he had access to a large supply of bull testicles in the Chicago

Doctors use steroid treatments, including injections, to treat chronic pain and other medical conditions.

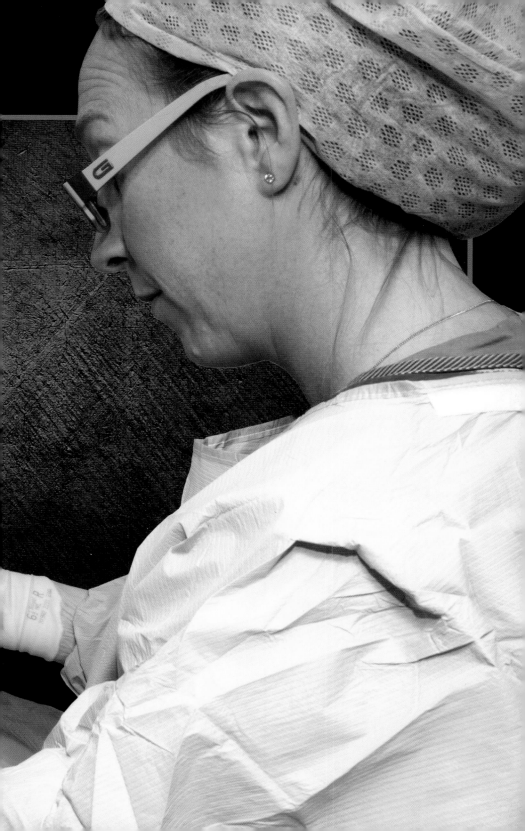

STEROID TREATMENT FOR ANIMALS

In veterinary medicine, steroids are used to treat pets such as cats and dogs as well as larger animals such as cattle and horses. Animals may be given corticosteroids if they lack energy or if their gums look pale. These are symptoms of anemia, a condition that occurs when there are not enough red blood cells to transport oxygen through the animal's body. One of the most common corticosteroids used to treat anemia in dogs is prednisone. Corticosteroids may also be used on animals to control inflammation or to treat allergies.

stockyards, where livestock were slaughtered for food. He and a student, Lemuel McGee, found a way to extract testosterone from bull testicles and use it in experiments to test the effects of this hormone. They first removed the testicles from a rooster. After several weeks, the bird's red comb had shrunk and become pale, as had the bird's wattles, or the loose skin at its throat. After being injected with the bull testosterone for two weeks, the bird's comb and wattles returned to the normal bright red of an unaltered rooster.

Scientists continued to research testosterone after Koch and McGee's experiments. In 1935, the German chemist Adolf Butenandt discovered the chemical structure of testosterone. Because cholesterol has the same basic chemical structure as testosterone, he was able to chemically synthesize testosterone from cholesterol. Following this discovery,

McGee and other university students processed 40 pounds (18 kg) of bull testicles to obtain 0.2 grams of testosterone.[1]

the earliest commercially made steroids were synthesized from cholesterol.

Steroids are most easily manufactured by altering one steroid to create another. Because of this, early AAS were synthesized from testosterone. The modifications were designed to enhance testosterone's muscle-building abilities. Today, most steroids are manufactured from chemical compounds found in plants and fungi. These compounds are chemically similar to cholesterol in animals and humans. In plants, they are called phytosterols. In fungi, they are called ergosterols. They can be converted into steroids that people can use.

Rhizopus nigricans, or black bread mold, is one type of fungus that is used to manufacture steroids.

TESTOSTERONE BOOST

The primary medical use for AAS is to treat teenage and adult males whose bodies do not produce enough testosterone. Boys who are late to develop secondary sexual characteristics may have hypogonadism. This problem usually corrects itself with time, because increased testosterone production comes with puberty.

Researchers have discovered that the timing of puberty has a strong genetic component. In some cases, hypogonadism is hereditary, or passed down through a person's genes. In other cases, hypogonadism can be caused by an infection.

KLINEFELTER'S SYNDROME

A person's chromosomes carry a unique genetic code. Each cell in a person's body normally has 46 chromosomes. Two of these chromosomes determine the person's gender. Men normally have one X chromosome and one Y chromosome. Women normally have two X chromosomes. A man with Klinefelter's syndrome has two X chromosomes and one Y chromosome. Klinefelter's syndrome affects one in every 1,000 male infants.[2] One symptom of Klinefelter's syndrome is low testosterone. Boys with Klinefelter's syndrome will not experience the physical changes that come with puberty unless they receive TRT. This will allow their bodies to grow and develop, but most will remain infertile.

Hypogonadism in men can be treated with testosterone replacement therapy (TRT). People who receive TRT are given low doses of testosterone. Testosterone can be given as injections or in other forms, such as gels or patches. The goal is to replace just enough testosterone to jump-start puberty. TRT can also be used to increase testosterone levels in people with other conditions, such as Klinefelter's syndrome.

Adult men can also experience low testosterone. Although a man's testosterone level drops gradually starting in his early twenties, some men's testosterone drops more quickly than it should. This can happen because they are obese, drink too much alcohol, have high blood pressure or cholesterol, or abuse AAS. When a person takes AAS and exceeds a normal amount of testosterone, his body reduces its own production of the hormone to try to return testosterone levels to normal. When

Other symptoms of Klinefelter's syndrome include language and learning difficulties.

the person quits taking AAS, his body may still produce too little testosterone.

Certain medical conditions can also result in low testosterone. These include a tumor in the pituitary gland or hypothalamus. A tumor is an abnormal growth of tissue. The pituitary gland and hypothalamus help control the production of hormones, including testosterone. Other causes of low testosterone include diabetes, certain cancer treatments, or injuries to the testicles.

DANGEROUS IMPORTS

Most AAS that are sold illegally in the United States have been smuggled in from China, Mexico, or various European countries. These countries have different drug laws than the United States. Smugglers can more easily acquire steroids in these places. Many smuggled steroids arrive in the United States in the form of a powder and are mixed with various additives before they are sold. Mixing in additives gives the smuggler more product to sell. These additives can include baby oil, vegetable oil, peanut oil, sesame oil, motor oil, or even horse urine. Smugglers also sell counterfeit AAS, which are fake and often do not contain active steroids. Health officials warn people not to buy steroids on the black market because the sellers have no reason to reveal what they are adding to dilute the steroids. Because of this, people do not really know what they are buying and putting into their bodies. A small amount of illegally sold steroids in the United States are stolen from pharmacies.

Low testosterone can lead to many changes in a man's body. These include loss of muscle mass and rapid weight gain. A man with low testosterone may also have problems functioning sexually or notice male-pattern baldness. He may also have problems sleeping, develop persistent fatigue, or suffer from depression. These are the same symptoms that occur in an older man as his testosterone level drops with age.

Although testosterone is considered a male hormone, females also produce it. In a woman, low testosterone decreases sex drive and lowers the production of new blood cells. Low testosterone levels in women can be caused by a damaged ovary or ovarian dysfunction. Doctors may prescribe a course of TRT to treat low testosterone in these cases. Testosterone is also given in hormone therapy undertaken by a transgender person who was assigned female at birth as a part of a transition to a male expression of gender. Prescription testosterone can be administered as a patch sold under the brand name Androderm, as an injection such as Depo-testosterone, or as a gel called AndroGel that is applied to and absorbed through the skin. Some patients may prefer patches or injection treatments because gels can rub off on other people.

PREVENTING WEIGHT LOSS

Doctors may also prescribe AAS to treat weight loss in patients with acquired immunodeficiency syndrome (AIDS). The human immunodeficiency virus (HIV) causes AIDS. This virus attacks CD4 cells, which are the cells that fight infection in the body's immune system. This leaves the person vulnerable to infection. People with HIV may develop AIDS over time if their amount of CD4 cells drops too low. This can severely damage the immune system.

AAS AND HIV

Prescription doses of AAS can be used to treat weight loss in patients with HIV. But when injectable AAS are not used legally, the user is at risk of contracting HIV and developing AIDS. This is because some users of injectable AAS share both the AAS and the needles they use to inject the drugs. Someone who has HIV and uses a needle to inject AAS can pass the virus on to anyone else who uses the same unsterilized needle.

People with AIDS may lose both body fat and muscle. This loss of muscle and weight puts them at greater risk for muscle weakness and organ failure. Because AAS can increase muscle mass and cause weight gain, doctors may prescribe them to treat weight loss in AIDS patients. This treatment can help stabilize a patient's health.

Because they are used to treat many health conditions, AAS will continue to be available. When taken legally and in prescribed doses as a medication, AAS can help improve the health of people with certain illnesses or health conditions. But, as is the case with many drugs that can be prescribed legally, AAS are subject to abuse.

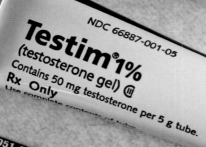

CHAPTER FOUR

SELF-PRESCRIBING

In the summer of 2000, American track-and-field athlete Marion Jones had just set a record as the first woman to earn five medals in a single Olympic Games. She had won three gold medals and two bronze medals in track events at the Sydney Olympics. People called her "the fastest woman alive."[1]

But federal investigators were suspicious. In 2001, Jones met with federal prosecutors who were looking into athletes and the use of PEDs. They showed Jones a vial of liquid. She recognized it as the supplement her coach had been giving her. The investigators told her it was an AAS known as "the clear" and

US track-and-field athlete Marion Jones celebrates a win in the 100-meter race at the 2000 Olympics.

asked whether she had ever taken it. Because she did not know her coach was giving her an AAS and wanted to avoid trouble, she told the investigators she had never used it. But in 2004, investigators spoke to shot-putter C. J. Hunter, who was Jones's ex-husband. He had tested positive for AAS in Sydney when the pair was married. In the interview, Hunter said that he had injected Jones with the clear.

Officials weren't only looking at the athletes. They were also investigating drug companies that might have provided AAS to the athletes. One of these companies was Bay Area Laboratory Co-operative (BALCO). BALCO founder Victor Conte testified that he had sat beside Jones and watched her inject herself with an AAS. He said she knew what it was.

In court, Jones admitted to taking AAS as she prepared for the Olympics. She was convicted not only of illegally using AAS but also of perjury, or lying to the investigators, and was sent to prison for six months. The IOC stripped Jones of the medals she had won in Sydney.

THE IOC SPEAKS OUT

The IOC did more than take back the medals Jones had won in Atlanta. It also banned Jones from attending the 2008 Beijing Olympic Games as a coach, reporter, or official of any kind. Jacques Rogge, then-president of the IOC, explained the IOC's actions: "I still think that this is a good thing for the fight against doping. The more athletes we can catch, the more credible we are, the more deterrent effect we will have and the more we are going to protect clean athletes."[2] The IOC takes the fight against doping seriously and wants to make a place in competitive sports for athletes who compete clean.

In a 2008 interview after her release from prison, Jones said, "I know I had worked hard, and I know I've been blessed with a great amount of talent. But I didn't know in my heart of hearts how much [the drug] aided me . . . how much that assisted me at the Sydney Games."[4]

In 2004, Marion Jones filed a $25 million lawsuit against Victor Conte, accusing him of trying to ruin her reputation and career.[3]

BUILDING MUSCLE

Many athletes are willing to risk getting caught because AAS provide an effective way to quickly build muscle when paired with a workout. Without training, an AAS user's physical performance may not improve. This is because when an athlete

Athletes can increase muscle mass naturally through exercise.

AAS VERSUS NATURAL

In 1996, a group of US doctors and scientists tested how much of a difference AAS make in muscle growth. They recruited a group of men and split them into four groups. One control group did not exercise or use AAS. One group received weekly 600-mg testosterone injections but did not exercise, while another group exercised but did not take any AAS. Another group both exercised and received weekly testosterone injections. For ten weeks, the men all followed the same diet. The two groups that worked out did the same weight training exercises. Not surprisingly, the men who did not exercise or take testosterone injections did not gain any muscle. The men who received testosterone injections but did not exercise gained an average of 7 pounds (3.2 kg) of muscle each. Those who worked out but did not take testosterone injections gained an average of 4 pounds (1.8 kg) of muscle each. The men who worked out and received testosterone injections gained an average of 13 pounds (5.9 kg) of muscle.[5] This additional muscle mass would give an athlete an edge over non-AAS-using competitors.

lifts weights, runs, or otherwise works a muscle, tiny tears appear in the muscle fibers. This is a natural part of working a muscle hard. The body immediately sets to work repairing these tears with proteins. Adding proteins makes the cells larger, leading to bigger and stronger muscle fibers. This is how athletes can add muscle mass over time.

Because one of the driving forces behind this rebuilding process is testosterone, AAS accelerate the speed at which this happens. AAS travel through the athlete's bloodstream and enter the muscle cells. The AAS bind with parts of the cells known as androgen receptors. The AAS use these receptors to accelerate protein production and muscle growth. Different AAS work at different rates and can result in enormous

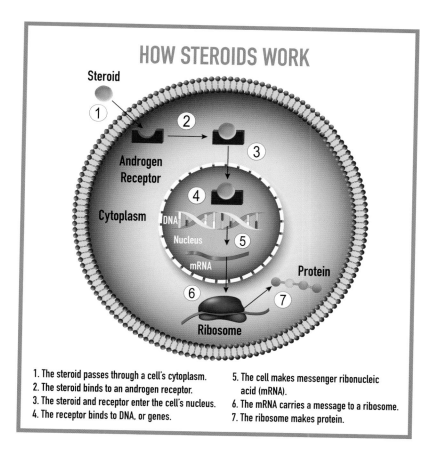

HOW STEROIDS WORK

Steroid

1

2

Androgen
Receptor

3

Cytoplasm

4

DNA

Nucleus

5

mRNA

Protein

6

7

Ribosome

1. The steroid passes through a cell's cytoplasm.
2. The steroid binds to an androgen receptor.
3. The steroid and receptor enter the cell's nucleus.
4. The receptor binds to DNA, or genes.

5. The cell makes messenger ribonucleic acid (mRNA).
6. The mRNA carries a message to a ribosome.
7. The ribosome makes protein.

bodybuilder muscles or the toned, lean muscles of a runner. The rate at which AAS work depends on many factors, including the type of steroid used, the dose, and how long it circulates in the body. The result the athlete desires depends on the sport and the athlete's individual goals.

Many professional athletes who turn to AAS do so because of the expectations that come along with signing bonuses and lucrative contracts. That was the reasoning behind the decision made by baseball player Alex Rodriguez, who played for the

Seattle Mariners, the Texas Rangers, and the New York Yankees over the course of 22 seasons. He explained that his $252 million contract caused "an enormous amount of pressure . . . to perform at a high level every day."[6] A baseball player such as Rodriguez goes for a leaner muscle mass, whereas a bodybuilder would be looking for bulk.

Some athletes abuse AAS to achieve faster recovery times. An athlete's body releases cortisol during exercise. Cortisol breaks down muscle tissue and causes sore muscles. AAS can keep cortisol from binding to its receptors. Blocking this binding process helps minimize the breakdown of muscle tissue and hastens recovery time.

STACKING AND PYRAMIDING

An individual athlete may experiment with different combinations of AAS. This process is known as stacking because athletes who dope often "stack" one drug on another, or take multiple drugs at the same time. Sometimes they stack a combination of oral and injected AAS. Oral AAS are taken by mouth, usually in pill form. An athlete who abuses AAS may stack a combination of AAS for a period, stop using AAS for a short time, and then repeat this process. This behavior is called cycling. Between cycles of AAS, the athlete may use a non-steroid drug, such as Clomid or tamoxifen. These drugs boost the user's testosterone level until the next cycle of AAS. Clomid is an oral prescription drug commonly used to treat infertility. Tamoxifen is a prescription drug commonly used to treat breast cancer in men and women. Both drugs increase the user's testosterone levels.

Another technique athletes use is called pyramiding. Athletes who pyramid may start using one type of AAS and slowly add others or increase their dosage, reaching a high point in the middle of their cycle before tapering off again. Although the effects of these techniques have not been scientifically proven, athletes experiment and exchange information looking for the end results they want.

NOT JUST THE JOCKS

Not all people who abuse AAS are athletes. Some experts note that the abuse of AAS today has become increasingly common among the general public. Dr. Shalender Bhasin, the director of the Research Program in Men's Health at Brigham and Women's Hospital, headed an expert panel on PEDs that met under the direction of the Endocrine Society in 2013. Bhasin stated,

STACKING

Although AAS are the most abused category of drugs among athletes, some bodybuilders stack a variety of substances. They may abuse diuretics, or drugs that cause the user to urinate more frequently, to mask their abuse of AAS. Diuretics dilute urine, which makes the amount of testosterone in the urine seem lower. Bodybuilders may also stack thyroid medications such as Cytomel, Triacana, and Synthroid. These drugs regulate a person's metabolism. Bodybuilders who stack with thyroid medications believe these drugs will increase the muscle-building properties of AAS. Some bodybuilders have stacked 10 to 15 drugs at a time.

"Nearly all of the nonathlete anabolic steroid users are male [recreational] weight lifters."[7] These men lift weights to improve their appearance. They experience societal and peer pressure to be more muscular.

Among athletes, one group of people that are prone to AAS abuse is athletic trainers. In 2006, surveys of weight trainers in US gyms and health clubs found that approximately 15 to 30 percent of those surveyed had abused AAS.[8] Researchers believe that unrealistic body standards promoted by the media make people more likely to develop body image issues. People who have body image issues, including athletes and athletic trainers, may turn to AAS or other unhealthy habits to achieve the results they want.

Eventually, many of these recreational users of AAS notice the toll AAS take on their bodies. When Dr. Bhasin sees signs in a patient that might indicate AAS abuse, he asks the person if they have been using AAS. Bhasin said, "I can't recall the last time a patient didn't tell me

AAS ABUSE AMONG PERFORMERS

Actors are also under great pressure to be muscular and fit. In Hollywood, the temptation to abuse AAS can be extreme, especially among middle-aged male actors who want to be able to compete for roles with younger actors. Sculpted muscles matter when it comes time for a close-up. Dancers and fashion models are also often under pressure to abuse AAS. They often find their physical appearance under scrutiny.

Athletes may feel pressure from their peers or society to gain muscle mass.

about their anabolic steroid use when asked in a nonjudgmental manner. The fact that the patient has come to a physician is in itself an indication that they are seeking help."[9] Many of these people have just started to realize and understand the negative side effects of AAS.

CHAPTER FIVE

ANABOLIC STEROIDS TAKE A TOLL

In 2003, US teenager Dionne decided to take AAS because she wanted to be thinner. The 17-year-old high school cheerleader wanted six-pack abs she saw on some models in an athletics magazine. Her goal was to be a size 0, but skipping meals and forcing herself to throw up had not dropped enough weight to get her there. She talked to a friend on her school's football team and was able to get some AAS. After five weeks of using the AAS

Teenagers with body image issues may abuse AAS to achieve weight loss goals.

Winstrol, she had gained 8 pounds (3.6 kg), and her voice had deepened.

As the artificial hormones course through their veins, people develop several visible signs of AAS abuse, such as weight gain due to fluid retention. Other side effects include changes in mood, which may be harder to spot. But both mental and physical side effects can be serious if not treated.

HORMONE PROBLEMS

AAS influence secondary sexual characteristics for both men and women. Although Dionne did not report experiencing these changes, female users often see an increase in body hair, and their skin becomes rougher. Many women also notice a reduction in the size of their breasts and an enlargement of their clitoris. Women who abuse AAS may also notice that their periods become less regular. These changes may be reversed after a woman stops taking AAS.

HIDING STEROID ABUSE

Dionne told reporters she easily hid her steroid abuse from her parents. She injected Winstrol once every other day and could easily do this in the bathroom. She believes that one reason she was able to hide her steroid abuse was that no one expected a girl to be on AAS to improve her looks. Dr. Linn Goldberg, head of health promotion and sports medicine at Oregon Health and Science University, says that girls are more likely to hide their steroid abuse than boys. "That's the difference between girls and boys, and how they use drugs," he said.[1]

Male abusers of AAS also see changes in their secondary sexual characteristics. The excess testosterone in their bodies is converted into estrogen. As a result, many of these men and boys develop enlarged breasts and nipples. This enlargement, known as gynecomastia, does not reverse itself if the person stops using AAS. It can only be corrected surgically. In addition to developing more breast tissue,

AAS abuse during a mother's pregnancy can cause the premature development of male features in her fetus.

men are likely to see their testicles and penis shrink. Their sperm production also decreases. If a man stops taking AAS, these changes can be reversed after several months. Unfortunately, other negative side effects of AAS are often invisible and can be deadly.

HEART HEALTH

AAS can damage a person's cardiovascular system in several ways. AAS increase the amount of low-density lipoproteins (LDLs) in a person's blood. LDL is often called "bad cholesterol." LDLs combine with and transport fats in the bloodstream. Increased amounts of these proteins mean more fats can enter the bloodstream and clog an artery.

This problem can be aggravated by oral AAS, which reduce the amount of high-density lipoprotein (HDL) in the user's blood. HDL is often called "good cholesterol." HDL picks up excess fat

Androstenedione and other AAS have been linked to heart disease and other health problems.

in the bloodstream and carries it to the liver. The liver produces a digestive juice that breaks down the fat so it can be absorbed in the bloodstream. Lower levels of HDL result in more fat in the bloodstream.

Although the blood normally produces proteins that dissolve blood clots, AAS minimize the production of these proteins.

They also make platelets in the blood more likely to stick to each other, forming a cluster that can lead to a clot. Eventually, these clots can lead to a heart attack.

AAS can also cause vasospasms, or the narrowing of arteries that occurs when blood vessels spasm. A vasospasm can occur in and affect any part of the body. AAS make it harder for the chemical nitric oxide to relax the blood vessels. Nitric oxide is produced within the arteries. When this chemical can no longer relax the blood vessels, the vessels eventually spasm. In the coronary artery, the artery that supplies blood to the heart, a vasospasm can cause chest pains. If not treated promptly, it can lead to a heart attack.

When vasospasms occur in the brain, people have stroke-like symptoms. These include slurred speech, confusion, weakness on one side of the body, trouble walking, headaches, and dizziness.

MIKE MATARAZZO

Mike Matarazzo was a world-class bodybuilder who placed in competitions from 1989 to 1998. He abused AAS throughout his bodybuilding career. In 2004, he underwent triple bypass surgery to repair clogged arteries. Matarazzo had thought that his fitness level would assure him of a long, healthy life. Too late, he realized he was wrong. "There's no way you can do those things and guarantee safety," said Matarazzo. "Furthermore, I was on the lighter end of the scale. . . . I had opportunities to do a lot more to myself chemically, but I didn't; yet, I still got hurt."[2] After his triple bypass surgery, Matarazzo was no longer able to compete in bodybuilding competitions. He continued to have heart problems, including another heart attack in 2007. On August 16, 2014, the 48-year-old died of a heart attack while awaiting a heart transplant.

These effects can take place singly or in combination, leading to a heart attack or stroke.

OTHER SIDE EFFECTS

A serious side effect associated with AAS taken orally is liver damage. Oral AAS are more damaging to the liver than other forms of AAS because users tend to take them in higher doses. Oral AAS are also designed to be harder to digest than other forms of AAS. The liver breaks down nutrients so the human body can use them. It also filters out and breaks down harmful substances within the body. Because the liver cannot easily break down AAS, these steroids damage the liver and cause a condition known as cholestasis. In cholestasis, a digestive fluid called bile builds up in the liver because it is not passing into the intestines as it should. Bile that builds up may eventually leak into the bloodstream. Symptoms that show this has occurred include dark urine, nausea, loss of appetite, and jaundice, or a yellowing of the skin and eyes.

AAS that are taken orally have also been shown to cause

BONE FUSION

AAS abuse may cause stunted growth in young users. AAS can fuse, or close, the growth centers in bones. These centers are the points from which bones lengthen when a child or teen grows. Dr. Gary Wadler, a New York University School of Medicine professor and an expert on the effects of AAS abuse, said, "Once these growth plates are closed, they cannot reopen so adolescents that take too many (anabolic) steroids may end up shorter than they should have been."[3]

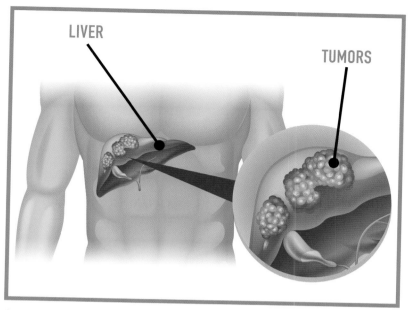

LIVER

TUMORS

AAS taken as pills may cause noncancerous tumors to grow on the user's liver.

noncancerous tumors in the liver. These tumors can rupture and lead to bleeding in the liver, which can be fatal. Liver cancer may also be linked to oral AAS abuse, but doctors and scientists are still looking for supporting evidence.

Other well-known side effects of AAS include mood swings and outbursts of anger. These emotional changes are commonly referred to as roid rage. Dionne told reporters that after five weeks, she became angry and short tempered. Other people who have abused AAS have reported that they became aggressive and violent. This may lead them to get into fights or, in some cases, commit crimes such as armed robbery, burglary, and vandalism.

ROID RAGE

Scientists are still attempting to identify the cause-and-effect link between AAS and roid rage. In a 2006 study, researchers at Northeastern University studied the effects of AAS in hamsters. They gave a group of more than 100 hamsters AAS injections and examined the hamsters' behavior compared with a control group of hamsters that didn't receive AAS. The hamsters that received AAS were more likely to attack other hamsters than the hamsters that didn't receive AAS. The researchers found evidence that these effects may be long lasting. Even weeks after they'd stopped giving AAS to the hamsters, most of them still behaved aggressively.[4]

In 2005, researcher Lena Lundholm headed a group of scientists who looked at AAS and other drug abuse among 10,365 Swedish men. They found a link between abuse of AAS and abuse of other drugs, such as amphetamines. Lundholm's group also noted a link between the abuse of AAS and violent criminal behavior. She concluded that the combination of many drugs, not just AAS, may cause violent behavior.[5]

Roid rage isn't the only mental problem experienced by people who abuse AAS. Some suffer from delusions or mania. A delusion is a false belief that a person considers to be true. When someone has a delusion, the person loses touch with reality. One common delusion that people who abuse AAS may have is that they are invincible. When someone else challenges this idea, users may go into a roid rage. Users who suffer from mania are highly energetic, impulsive, and paranoid. They often feel as if someone is out to get them. Both delusions and mania can lead to conflicts with other people.

Another common side effect among people who abuse AAS is skin infections. AAS stimulate the production of extra skin lubricants. These fatty oils

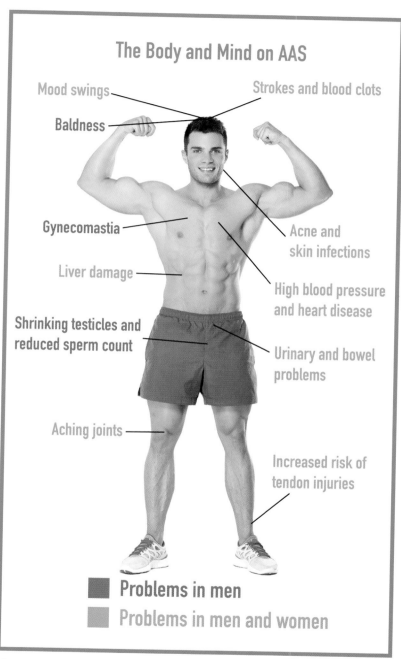

The Body and Mind on AAS

Mood swings

Strokes and blood clots

Baldness

Gynecomastia

Acne and skin infections

Liver damage

Shrinking testicles and reduced sperm count

High blood pressure and heart disease

Urinary and bowel problems

Aching joints

Increased risk of tendon injuries

■ Problems in men
■ Problems in men and women

Men and women who abuse AAS may notice mental and physical side effects.

feed bacteria on the skin. Excess lubricants mean that bacteria flourish, which contributes to skin infections. Far worse than acne, these infections can become tumor-like growths that, even when healed, often leave scars.

Some evidence suggests that abusing AAS also increases an athlete's risk of tendon injury. Because the user's body doesn't need all of the testosterone provided by the steroid, some of the testosterone is converted to estradiol, a type of estrogen. This conversion interferes with the formation of collagen. Collagen is a protein in skin and tendons. When someone takes AAS, tendons become stiffer. The strength of the tendon is not affected, so scientists are unsure why this leads to tendon rupture. The problem may be that the surrounding muscle does become stronger, leaving the tendon unable to resist the increased strain.

These side effects and health concerns are the reasons doctors and lawmakers worry about the number of people abusing AAS. Although some of the effects, including skin infections, mental health issues, and even minor liver damage, are reversible, strokes and heart attacks leave permanent damage even when they are not fatal. Despite this, many people disregard the negative effects because these effects build up slowly over time.

IF YOU USE STEROIDS, THESE AREN'T THE ONLY THINGS STACKED AGAINST YOU.

CHAPTER SIX

STEROIDS AND THE LAW

In 1975, the IOC added AAS to their list of banned substances. The committee believed athletes who took AAS had an unfair advantage over those who did not. The IOC was also concerned with keeping athletes healthy because there are risks associated with AAS abuse.

Despite these valid reasons to ban AAS, passing legislation in the United States to control AAS was controversial. The Drug Enforcement Administration (DEA) objected to including AAS in the Controlled Substance Act (CSA). The CSA is the federal drug policy of the United States. It regulates the manufacture, import, sale, possession, and use of stimulants, AAS, and other drugs.

Victor Conte, *above*, holds a photo of baseball player Barry Bonds. Conte was arrested in 2005 for providing steroids to athletes.

In a 1988 hearing, DEA Deputy Assistant Administrator Gene Haislip told members of the US Congress that the CSA was meant to control substances that are taken because of their effects on the user's mind. Because AAS are taken to develop the body, Haislip believed they should not be added to the list of controlled substances. He told Congress he was also worried that, with the widespread use of AAS, adding them to the ban would create too much work for the DEA, the principal agency charged with enforcing any ban. "We do, in fact, have our hands full with some other problems," Haislip said.[1]

The DEA wasn't the only group that spoke out against a ban. The American Medical Association (AMA) also fought against a proposed ban. In the spring of 1989, Dr. Edward Langston, a representative for the AMA, told a Senate committee not to include AAS in any ban because they are used to treat several ailments. He also believed there was no clear evidence that AAS were addictive, so it would be a mistake to lump them in with highly addictive drugs.[2]

Congress agreed with those who thought AAS represented a widespread and dangerous problem. For this reason, it decided to include AAS in the CSA. But AAS abuse continued to grow. Lawmakers blamed this growth on the limited number of substances affected by the original wording of the CSA. Because of this, when the Anabolic Steroid Control Act was drafted in

JOE BIDEN'S ROLE

Senator Joe Biden coauthored the original Anabolic Steroid Control Act of 1990 with another senator, Strom Thurmond. When AAS abuse continued to grow and extended beyond professional athletes to the general public, Biden coauthored another bill. Working with Senator Orrin Hatch, Biden coauthored the Anabolic Steroids Control Act of 2004. This added another group of AAS and steroid supplements to the Schedule III list. This bill was popular in both Congressional houses. Lawmakers wanted to see an end to the abuse of AAS and the health risks they posed. President George W. Bush signed the bill into law on October 22, 2004.

2004 under the direction of Senator Joe Biden, an additional 26 AAS were added to the Drug Schedules.

THE DRUG SCHEDULES

The CSA divides controlled substances into five groups. These groups are called schedules. A drug is put into a schedule category depending on how addictive it is and whether it has medical uses.

Schedule I drugs have no widely accepted medical uses, and doctors cannot prescribe them. They are highly addictive. The Schedule I list includes heroin and peyote. Marijuana is also considered a Schedule I drug because of its addictive tendencies, although it has been legalized in Colorado and Washington State for recreational purposes. Marijuana can also be prescribed in a number of states, including California, for medical reasons, including as a painkiller.

All Schedule II drugs have accepted medical uses. But because the drugs are highly addictive, they are likely to be abused. Cocaine, methamphetamine, and the painkiller oxycodone are all Schedule II drugs.

AAS are Schedule III drugs. Drugs in this category are addictive but not as highly addictive as the drugs in Schedules I and II. Schedule III drugs include codeine, a pain reliever and cough suppressant. Doctors can prescribe Schedule III drugs, so they are available for patients who need them. Because AAS are essential to the well-being of certain patients, they are on this list.

Schedule IV and Schedule V drugs are less addictive still. These drugs have medical uses. Schedule IV drugs include benzodiazepines, a category that includes sedatives. Among the Schedule V drugs are prescription cough suppressants and mild prescription pain relievers, both of which might be abused if not taken under the direction of a doctor.

CHANGING LAWS

The purpose of drug schedules is to make passing legislation easier at the state level. When a state passes a drug law, the text does not have to list every single drug to which the law applies. Instead, the text has to include only the appropriate schedule. This makes it easier to write laws. A drug can also be added to a category without having to rewrite laws in every state. This meant that when additional AAS were added to Schedule III in 2004, the state laws involving Schedule III AAS did not have to be rewritten.

THE LAW AND SPORTS BANS

Because AAS are Schedule III substances, it is illegal to have or sell them without a doctor's prescription. In the United States, if someone is convicted of possessing AAS illegally and it is a first offense, the person can be fined up to $1,000. He or she may also spend up to one year in prison.[4]

If someone is convicted of selling AAS illegally, the penalties are much higher. In the United States, a first offense can bring a fine of up to $250,000 and five years in prison.[6] The fine and prison time double for a second offense. These are the federal penalties. Anyone who is convicted of possession or distribution of AAS may face state penalties as well.

Athletes who are caught using AAS often face discipline from sports organizations. The NCAA banned AAS for the same reasons the IOC did: because AAS give an athlete an unfair advantage and because they can damage the athlete's health.

VICTOR CONTE

In 2005, Victor Conte spent four months in prison. Conte was the founder and president of BALCO, a pharmaceutical company that provided AAS to athletes without prescriptions. After his release from prison, he told reporters that officials will continue to find it difficult to catch athletes who abuse AAS.[3] New, faster-acting AAS leave the body more quickly and may not be detected by the tests currently available.

In Texas, someone caught with 400 grams or more of an AAS may receive a life sentence and a fine of up to $50,000.[5]

College athletes who are caught using AAS may have to forfeit medals and records, and they may be banned from competition. State sporting associations have similar penalties for younger students who test positive for AAS. In New Jersey, for example, high school students caught abusing AAS are ineligible to play sports for one year. They also forfeit any honors or awards earned while taking AAS.

Many professional sports organizations, such as the National Football League and the National Hockey League, have also put steroid bans into place. Perhaps the biggest scandal took place in Major League Baseball (MLB). Although MLB had a steroid ban starting in 1991, no league-wide system of testing was put into place until 2003. This meant that players were unlikely to get caught. People were suspicious about the number of players who might be abusing AAS. Many MLB players were not only sporting huge muscles but also were breaking records in unprecedented numbers.

PITCHERS IN TROUBLE

In 2015, four MLB pitchers received 80-game suspensions: Arodys Vizcaíno, David Rollins, Ervin Santana, and Jenrry Mejía. All four of these pitchers tested positive for the AAS stanozolol. This was the same type of steroid that was abused by Canadian sprinter Ben Johnson. When his doping was discovered, Johnson lost his gold medal and world record in the 100-meter dash at the 1988 Olympics in Seoul, South Korea. Despite the history of athletes being caught abusing this and other types of AAS, players still give in to the pressure to abuse AAS to bulk up.

In 2011, Barry Bonds admitted to abusing steroids during his MLB career.

One of these records was the number of players to hit 50 home runs in a single season. From 1961 to 1994, only three players had achieved this goal. But in 1996, Mark McGwire of the Oakland Athletics missed part of the season and still hit 52 home runs. The following year, both McGwire and the Seattle Mariners' Ken Griffey Jr. nearly broke the 1961 record of 61 home runs in a season, hitting 58 and 56 home runs, respectively. During the 1997 season, 13 MLB players hit at least 40 home runs apiece. Fans watched McGwire, who then played for the

KIT NUMBER

Please ensure that the kit number above corresponds with the number on the kit inside

DOPING CONTROL KIT

Tel: UK +44 (0) 181 333 536A
Fax: UK +44 (0) 181 311 0423

Versapak

ING CONTI
Comi

St. Louis Cardinals, and Sammy Sosa of the Chicago Cubs. Both approached the 1961 home run record, and McGwire broke it when he hit both his sixty-first and sixty-second home runs in a single game. When the season ended, Sosa had 66 home runs to McGwire's 70.[7] Barry Bonds, another heavy hitter, hit 73 home runs in the 2001 season.[8]

Many fans and MLB officials were suspicious. A deal was negotiated with the players' union. In 2003, MLB officials began testing players for AAS. If more than 5 percent of players tested positive, more serious testing and penalties would be put in place the next year. These penalties would range from counseling for a first offense to a one-year suspension for a fifth offense. Approximately 5 to 7 percent of the tests came back positive.[9] Regular mandatory testing was initiated in 2004 because of these results.

Even while sports organizations and law enforcement agencies work to stop illegal steroid use, AAS continue to be a problem. Athletes feel pressured to use every means possible to excel. Nonathletes who abuse AAS often do so to meet the standards of physical perfection set by society.

CHAPTER SEVEN

PRESSURE TO USE

In 2016, the University of Michigan surveyed approximately 50,000 US teenagers about their illegal drug use. This annual survey, funded by the National Institute on Drug Abuse (NIDA), asked the teenagers whether they had ever taken steroids without a doctor's prescription. Approximately 650 teenagers, or 1.3 percent, answered "yes." According to the survey, teenage use of other drugs, such as marijuana, is higher.[1] Still, many experts recognize that AAS abuse is a problem among high school students. And although many people think of AAS as boys' or men's drugs, girls and women dope, too. Today, teenage girls are the fastest-growing group of AAS users.

Teenage or young adult athletes may feel pressure to use AAS to improve their athletic performance.

TYLER HAMILTON

In 2010, Tyler Hamilton, a former teammate of cyclist Lance Armstrong, was called before a Senate investigative committee to testify about doping in sports. He decided to admit to doping. For the first time, he told the truth about himself and talked about seeing other cyclists dope. The surprise for Hamilton was the difference he felt going into the hearing and coming out. "It was almost a bit spiritual, really. It was just a huge weight coming off my shoulders."[2] After testifying to the grand jury, he agreed to speak to *60 Minutes,* a televised news program, about the investigation. Before the interview aired, he talked to his family and admitted that earlier allegations and positive drug tests were true. His family has a history of depression. Hamilton himself had been taking antidepressants to treat his depression for ten years. Without the lies, the pressure he had created for himself no longer added to his mental health problems. Although he still has what he calls "quiet periods" when he has no interest in socializing, he no longer needs antidepressants to function.[4]

According to many experts, the primary reason teens turn to AAS is because they feel pressured. Tyler Hamilton, anti-doping advocate and former professional cyclist, agrees with this. Hamilton educates young athletes about the dangers of PEDs. He knows the consequences of steroid abuse firsthand. He had to return his Olympic gold medal, won for cycling at the 2004 Olympics in Athens, Greece, after admitting to abusing AAS. Now, he speaks out against doping of all kinds.

"What I encounter when talking to teens is the significant pressure they feel to excel," said Hamilton. "Whether it's in sports, school, social status, or appearance, teens feel they need to be better."[3] It is often the people who should be offering teens unconditional

support, such as coaches, who
are heaping on the pressure.
Teens also often feel pressured
by the media, which bombards

them with images of thin and fit people who seemingly excel at everything they do.

POWERING UP

Although many people discuss the pressure teen girls are under to look perfect, many boys also feel this pressure. Girls frequently feel the need to compete with slender models, pop stars, and actresses. Boys are competing against images of men with six-pack abs and massive muscles.

In July 2016, the journal *Pediatrics* found that by the age of 19, 12 percent of US males who participated in a study reported using a muscle-building product. These products included AAS. The study collected data from 7,840 boys, surveying them annually from 1996 to 2001 and every other year after that.[5] It found that males between the ages of 16 and 25 were three times as likely as younger males to have used a muscle-building product. Males who identified as homosexual were slightly more likely to try AAS. Researchers are unsure how gender conformity or sexual orientation may factor into trying AAS or other products that might alter a user's appearance.

Although female athletes may abuse AAS, more often teen girls who take AAS do it for reasons other than to be better competitors. When the US Centers for Disease Control and Prevention (CDC) surveyed teen girls in 2003, most of the girls who said they had taken AAS gave one of two reasons. Dr. Linn Goldberg was the lead researcher on a project that worked with the CDC's survey results. As she explained: "They [teen girls] take it [AAS] to get more lean body mass. Some take them [AAS] for protection—to get stronger."[6]

The idea that women may take AAS to protect themselves has been confirmed by scientific studies. In one 1999 study published in the journal *Comprehensive Psychiatry*, 75 female weightlifters were surveyed. Seven of the ten women who reported that they had been raped as teenagers or adults had abused AAS.[8] In another study, conducted by NIDA, researchers interviewed 75 female bodybuilders. Sixty-six percent of the bodybuilders

COPYCAT AAS USE

In a 2008 survey reported in the medical journal *Medicine & Science in Sports & Exercise*, high school students who took AAS were asked whether steroid abuse by professional athletes influenced their decision to use. Twenty percent said this did influence their decision. When asked the same question about friends who used AAS, 50 percent of respondents said that professional athletes' steroid abuse was a big influence on their friends.[7] This suggests that teens understand that their idols can be an influence, although they think other people are more susceptible than they are.

Some women take AAS because they think building muscle mass will protect them against sexual assault.

who admitted to taking AAS reported having been raped.[9] Compare this with the 19.6 percent of all US women who report having been raped, according to a 2011 CDC survey.[10] The female bodybuilders believed that being bigger and stronger would make them intimidating or unattractive, thus guarding them against future sexual assaults.

SCHOOL SPORTS

Like professional athletes, teenagers may also abuse AAS to perform well in a sport. In 2014, the Partnership for Drug-Free Kids, a nonprofit organization that educates the public about drug use within the United States, released a report that found that one in five teens knows at least one friend who takes steroids. According to the report, another one in five teens thinks it would be easy to buy steroids.[11] A big part of this prevalence is blamed on the culture of high school sports. Travis T. Tygart, CEO of the USADA, said: "We know that the win-at-all costs culture in sport and in society as a whole has a direct impact on the health and well-being of young people."[12]

It is not just coaches who are pressuring teens to excel in sports. Parents and teammates are just as influential at making teens believe everything relies on their athletic performance. This is especially true for a strong athlete who dreams of going to state or regional competitions, has hopes of making the Olympics, or is in the running for a college scholarship. This pressure on a teen is paired with the knowledge that he or she can likely get away with steroid abuse. In 2014, only 20 percent of US high schools had drug testing policies.[13] The risk of being caught is further reduced because the typical test looks for marijuana, amphetamines, opioids, cocaine, and phencyclidine (PCP). AAS go undetected. Teens are naturally inclined to take risks and experiment, and the

STATE TESTING

In 2016, only Illinois and New Jersey had statewide programs to test student athletes for AAS. During the 2015–2016 school year, New Jersey tested 497 samples from 343 male athletes and 154 female athletes and found zero positive samples.[14] Officials do not believe this means no high school athlete is abusing AAS. The samples were taken before championship competitions from a random sampling of student athletes, but the athletes knew when they might be tested and could avoid doping at those times.

comparatively low likelihood of getting caught using AAS may make these drugs attractive to many teens.

MUSCLE DYSMORPHIC DISORDER

Being pressured by other people is one among many reasons teens may turn to AAS. Some people who abuse AAS suffer from body disorders. One of these disorders is muscle dysmorphic disorder, also known as bigorexia or reverse anorexia. A person with anorexia cannot see how thin he or she is and obsesses about eating very little food and working out to lose weight. Similarly, people who have muscle dysmorphic disorder focus obsessively on eating and exercise. But instead of focusing on

People with muscle dysmorphic disorder have high rates of substance abuse, including AAS abuse.

getting thin, people with muscle dysmorphic disorder focus on gaining muscle. However, their perceptions of their bodies and their muscle mass do not match reality. Australian psychologist Scott Griffiths, who specializes in muscle dysmorphic disorder and eating disorders in males, said, "They can look you in the eye and tell you that they're small, even though they're huge."[15]

Although both men and women can have muscle dysmorphic disorder, it is more common in men. Researchers suspect this might be because the image of an ideal woman, as promoted by society and the media, is thin, whereas the ideal man is muscular. People who suffer from muscle dysmorphic disorder work out aggressively and obsess about their appearance as they work for lean muscle. They also worry about eating the wrong foods, or foods that they think will make them fat. Because of this, they

The average age people develop muscle dysmorphic disorder is 19 years old.

INTERVENTION

When family and friends try to encourage someone with muscle dysmorphic disorder to get help, they have to be careful what they say. People with muscle dysmorphic disorder typically have a paranoid belief that people are lying to them. If others tell people with muscle dysmorphic disorder that they really are very muscular, it feeds into this paranoia. People with this disorder may believe friends or family members just cannot see them the way they really are. Instead, health-care professionals encourage concerned family and friends to focus on the effect that excessive time at the gym is having on school, friends, family, and work.

often avoid social obligations, including parties or dinners. At the expense of family, friends, work, and school, they focus on achieving more muscle mass. They often turn to AAS to meet these goals.

Publicized athletic competitions, such as bodybuilding competitions, can promote unrealistic body standards.

CHAPTER EIGHT

ADDICTION AND WITHDRAWAL

Because AAS abusers do not get high, many people question whether these drugs are truly addictive. They make the point that people do not crave more and more of the drug to achieve the same effect. However, medical experts believe AAS are addictive because people who abuse them show other signs of addiction.

Some signs of addiction to AAS are behavioral, including the drive to continue to use the drugs even when friends and family beg the user to stop. People who abuse AAS also focus on drug use at the expense of other things. They spend extraordinary sums of money to get the types of AAS they want.

Don Hooton poses with a photo of his son, Taylor Hooton, in 2015. Taylor became depressed after AAS withdrawal and committed suicide.

Studies have shown that laboratory animals will give themselves exogenous steroids whenever they have the opportunity, much as they do with drugs that are known to be addictive. In a 2001 study, scientists offered a group of hamsters two choices: a water bottle filled with a testosterone mixture or a water bottle filled with only water. Scientists found that the hamsters preferred the water bottle filled with testosterone.[1] In a 2002 study, lab rats injected themselves with testosterone by continually pushing a button that released testosterone into their bloodstreams.[2]

Unfortunately, many people who abuse AAS are embarrassed by their addiction and do not want to reveal their problem to parents or friends. In one well-known case of AAS abuse, Taylor Hooton, a teenage baseball player in Plano, Texas, repeatedly denied he was using AAS when confronted by his parents. He may have tried to stop using on his own. This can be dangerous because withdrawal can lead to depression and suicidal thoughts in addition to the physical complications users experience when they go off the drug. Without the help of a doctor or medical professional, withdrawal symptoms can be difficult to manage. Doctors believe that Taylor experienced depression as a part of

In 2013, the NCAA surveyed approximately 21,000 student athletes about drug use. Among those who did not abuse AAS, only 5.1 percent said that the reason they did not dope was because they were worried about getting caught by a drug test.[3]

his withdrawal symptoms, which led him to commit suicide.

PHYSICAL AND MENTAL WITHDRAWAL

People who take AAS experience a variety of symptoms when they quit using the drugs. Physical symptoms include sleep problems that contribute to an overall feeling of fatigue, and joint pains and muscle aches are common. A person who is withdrawing from AAS often feels restless and has little or no appetite. Some people even experience nausea and vomiting.

Other withdrawal symptoms are emotional. These range from mood swings to anxiety. Some people also have difficulty focusing. Users who attempt to quit also experience cravings for the drug. But by far the most serious symptom of withdrawal

TAYLOR HOOTON

Taylor Hooton's brother had been a baseball pitcher in college, and his cousin had been a major league pitcher. Seventeen-year-old Taylor had a legacy to live up to, and he was expected to start for his high school baseball team in the fall of 2003. But on July 15, 2003, Taylor hung himself after being grounded by his parents, who did not know he was injecting AAS. They had suspected he was abusing AAS, but he denied it and passed a drug test. His parents later learned the test looked for recreational drugs, not AAS. After his death, they were told that a high school coach suggested he needed to bulk up. His psychiatrist also revealed that Taylor had had low self-esteem and worried he wasn't good enough. Looking back, his parents saw many signs of AAS abuse. These included a rapid, 30-pound (14 kg) weight gain, irritability, and anger. After Taylor's death, his parents established a foundation in his name to educate people about the dangers of steroid abuse.

Depression is a common symptom of AAS withdrawal.

from AAS is depression. Depression can sometimes lead to suicide, as happened with Taylor.

The main reason people go through withdrawal symptoms when they quit using AAS is because AAS supplement the testosterone in their bodies. While taking AAS, their bodies attempt to return their levels of testosterone to normal. To do this, the body reduces the amount of testosterone it produces on its own. When the person quits using AAS, the level of artificial testosterone in his body drops. The symptoms of withdrawal continue until the body returns to a normal level of testosterone production.

AAS WITHDRAWAL TIMELINE	
NUMBER OF DAYS OFF THE DRUG	COMMON SYMPTOMS
DAYS 1-2	HEADACHE, IRRITABILITY, NAUSEA
DAYS 3-5	DEPRESSION, ANXIETY, EXHAUSTION
DAYS 6-7	NAUSEA, ABDOMINAL PAIN, WEIGHT LOSS, INSOMNIA, DEPRESSION
WEEK 2	BY THIS TIME, MOST SYMPTOMS WILL BE TAPERING OFF

The timeline of withdrawal from AAS may vary depending on the type and dose of AAS taken and how long the user has taken them. But the average AAS withdrawal period is approximately two weeks.

PAIRED ILLNESS

People who have abused AAS may also be dealing with a paired illness. A paired illness is an illness that commonly occurs with another illness. People who are addicted to AAS often have body image or eating disorders. People who have such disorders believe that their body or appearance is seriously flawed. Some people who abuse AAS, especially athletes, may have eating disorders such as anorexia or bulimia nervosa. Anorexia is characterized by a fixation on low body weight along with habitual and obsessive exercise. Bulimia is characterized by bingeing and purging, wherein excess food is consumed and then purged through either vomiting or the use of a medication that makes it easier for food waste to pass through the body. People with eating disorders often also have body dysmorphic disorder, which causes them to perceive themselves as overweight. Whether they purge or starve

NOT JUST A WOMEN'S PROBLEM

Eating disorders are nothing new, but until recently, they were seldom diagnosed in men or boys. Today, anorexia has been diagnosed in boys as young as eight years old. Many experts believe the rise in these disorders in the male population results from the media messages sent to men and boys about their bodies. Boys feel pressure to be lean and muscular. These expectations are often aggravated during puberty, when boys have a tendency to compare their own developments and bodily changes with those of their peers.

themselves, they fail to see the results they want. Some then also turn to AAS to help them appear slimmer or more muscular.

Not everyone who abuses AAS has a body image or eating disorder. But people who do will need the help of mental health professionals trained in treating those disorders. With this help, they can work through their body image issues without adopting a new harmful behavior in place of steroid abuse.

According to the American College of Sports Medicine, men between the ages of 20 and 29 have between 14 and 17 percent body fat on average.[4] But a man with body dysmorphia may think he is not fit enough although he has only 8 percent body fat.[5]

TREATMENT OPTIONS

A variety of treatment options exist for someone who has made the decision to quit using AAS. Inpatient drug rehabilitation is often the top choice for people who need medication to get through the detox period. Inpatient treatment involves staying in a treatment facility for a period without leaving. This type of treatment is useful if the person has been abusing several substances or has a paired illness that requires treatment. Another benefit is that it takes the person out of her normal routine and can help her break her destructive habits.

Similar treatments are available through outpatient rehabilitation. Outpatient treatment differs from inpatient treatment in that it allows the person to live at home and attend school or go to work. It is a less expensive option than inpatient

Counseling is an important step in the treatment process for people overcoming steroid addiction.

DETOX

AAS detox is the process that occurs when AAS work their way out of a user's body. Sometimes, a doctor will prescribe medication to reduce the symptoms of withdrawal during this period. Another strategy is to "taper" or "taper down," which involves reducing the dose of AAS over time. Detoxing is never easy and should be undertaken with advice from a doctor.

care, but it also makes it easier for the person to stay in touch with friends who may have encouraged steroid abuse in the first place.

Another treatment option is group counseling. This treatment consists of regular group meetings with other people who have abused AAS. In these counseling sessions, which are led by a therapist or counselor, people discuss their recovery and any problems they may be having. Participants can offer each other a great deal of support because they all may be going through similar problems.

Other people benefit from individual therapy. This treatment option offers more one-on-one time with the counselor or therapist. The person seeking to stop using AAS gets more individual attention and is able to focus on her particular issues. She is then able to discuss possible solutions and how to work toward these solutions.

WAKE-UP CALL

High school cheerleader Dionne realized her doping habit was out of control when she began to feel depressed and suicidal. "Something made me say, 'I need to take myself to the hospital, I need some help,'" she told a *New York Times* reporter in 2008. She checked into a hospital and was put on a daylong suicide watch. "I went to a mental health facility for three days after that. They put me on antidepressants and it took a long time to get it (the AAS) out of my system," she said.[6] She hopes she can help today's teens make better decisions.

Former AAS abusers usually need to stay in therapy for several years to remain drug-free. Therapy gives them the support they need to build new habits that will help them resist the urge to go back to using AAS. Sooner or later, most people are tempted to relapse, or return to using AAS. It is vital for them to have a support network in place to prevent this from happening. Although AAS withdrawal is not easy, with the right tools and the desire to succeed, it is possible.

CHAPTER NINE

THE FIGHT CONTINUES

Nonprescription AAS are illegal to purchase and distribute in the United States, but this doesn't mean that they are impossible to find. Some people, including many people who lift weights to improve their appearance, can buy them at their gyms. These people might purchase AAS from a fellow gym user or trainer.

In May 2013, the US Customs and Border Patrol opened a package addressed to Richard Gray, a personal trainer in Edison, New Jersey. Inside, they found 110 containers of various AAS. After they searched his home, agents described the basement as looking like a pharmaceutical company warehouse. Shelves of

Police Commissioner Raymond Kelly announces the arrests of 24 people who sold and distributed illegal steroids from two New York City gyms in 2007.

steroid pills lined the walls. Gray was arrested for distributing steroids to buyers across the country.

Other more recent events illustrate how widespread AAS abuse is among the general population. On the morning of February 22, 2017, the DEA raided Iron Addicts, a popular gym in Miami, Florida. Agents searched a second-floor office, using sledgehammers to break through the walls. The gym's co-owner, Richard Rodriguez, had been storing AAS in this office. Rodriguez was charged with using his supplements company to import, manufacture, and distribute AAS. The company, called Wellness, Fitness and Nutrition Network, sold AAS in both pill and injectable forms. This side business had earned Rodriguez and his wife more than $2.3 million between January 2015 and October 2016.[1]

LEGAL OVERSEAS

Every country has its own laws on steroid use, purchase, distribution, and possession.

BRIAN CUBAN

At a gym, a former professional football player told 26-year-old recreational weightlifter Brian Cuban about a doctor who prescribed AAS for weight gain. Cuban received a prescription and saw quick results when he paired AAS with harder workouts. Then he noticed that he began to develop anger issues, and he quit. But he eventually went back to abusing AAS, which he bought through the black market at his gym. He later quit doping again, but he still has heart problems. Today, he is an eating-disorder and addiction-awareness advocate in Dallas, Texas. He worries about the impact of AAS on teens. "Steroids can destroy our youth," Cuban said in a 2016 interview.[2]

In the United Kingdom, people can own, import, and export AAS legally as long as the steroids are for the person's own personal use. But anyone who imports AAS and then sells them has to pay a fine. Sellers can also be sentenced to up to 14 years in prison. In this way, the law in the United Kingdom protects the user but not the seller of AAS.

In contrast, Australia has one of the strictest drug codes in the world. The maximum penalty for either possession or sale of AAS in Australia is 25 years in prison. In Australia, people can be arrested for ordering AAS online.

In some countries, AAS that are illegal in the United States are legal and openly purchased in pharmacies. This is the case in Thailand, India, Mexico, Colombia, Bulgaria, and Poland. But availability does not guarantee quality, purity, or safety. AAS may be legal and inexpensive overseas, but their sale in these countries is often unregulated. This means

Brian Cuban, a recreational weightlifter, estimated that he spent $500 a month on AAS.[3]

STEROID VACATIONS

Steroid vacations help users avoid the high prices of buying black-market AAS in their home countries. When people take steroid vacations, they travel to countries where AAS are legal, such as Thailand, India, or Mexico. In the foreign country, users walk into pharmacies and ask for the types of AAS they want to use. These AAS cost much less than what they would in a user's home country. Users then stack a combination of AAS during their trip. Health-care officials warn people considering these vacations that some overseas pharmacies sell AAS intended for veterinary use, which may not be safe for human beings.

A customs officer in Germany shows some of the anabolic substances seized from drug smugglers and dealers in 2003.

that people who buy AAS through the mail or travel overseas to purchase them cannot know for sure what they are buying.

SCHOOL TESTING

Another part of the public confusion about AAS comes from mixed messages sent by high schools. Even in schools that want to discourage their athletes from abusing AAS, money comes

into play. Student athletes sign contracts promising to be good students and not abuse alcohol or drugs. But most likely, the school is not going to test all of its student athletes to make sure they comply. It is simply too expensive to test all athletes for the wide range of substances they could conceivably be using.

In May 2015, Texas state lawmakers defunded the state's high school drug testing program. In the preceding eight years, more than 63,000 samples had been tested at a cost of $10 million. The first 19,000 tests resulted in only nine confirmed cases of AAS abuse.[4] Supporters said the program effectively discouraged students from abusing AAS. Critics called the program an ineffective waste of money.

Don Catlin, who conducted NCAA testing for the University of California, Los Angeles, explained that the Texas testing program found such a low number of steroid abuse cases because there were too many flaws in their system. The very first test looked for only ten different AAS, a fraction of those available. In subsequent tests, school officials had to be told when testers would visit a campus. Although this information is supposed to be confidential, it takes only one person to pass along a warning for the upcoming visit to become public knowledge. Because of this, the element of surprise was often lost, and athletes who abused AAS could plan to be absent or cheat. Cheating is often easy because minors must be given privacy when they provide a urine sample. This gives them the opportunity to substitute clean urine if their own might show evidence of steroid use.

State officials and schools want to protect the health and safety of their students. Unfortunately, they often do not have the money for comprehensive drug testing. They also lack the

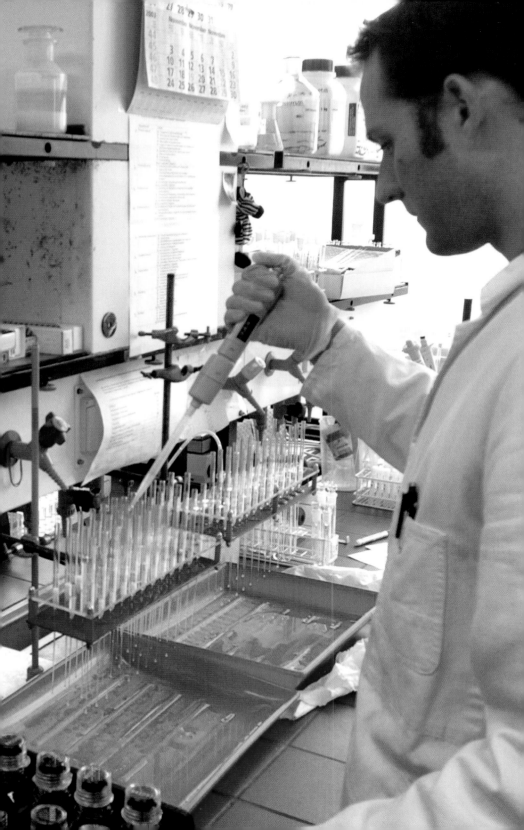

legal ability to guarantee that students are not substituting clean samples from other people.

LOSING MEDALS

Controversy continues to plague the Olympics and other sports competitions. The IOC continues to test athletes for AAS and other illegal substances. Unfortunately, people who are determined to abuse AAS can also be very good at avoiding detection. This can be fairly easy to do if they use recently developed drugs. In some cases, effective tests may not yet have been developed for these drugs. For example, the AAS tetrahydrogestrinone (THG) was developed by BALCO to be undetectable. A test to detect THG was developed only after a coach sent a syringe containing a few drops of the steroid to the USADA in 2003.

But tests do continue to improve. In 2007, Oral Turinabol could be detected in blood or urine only up to five to seven days after it was ingested. But with today's tests, this same steroid can be detected up to six months

NOT JUST THE RUSSIANS

Russia is not the only country in the Olympic Games whose athletes have abused steroids. United World Wrestling, the world governing body for wrestling, banned two wrestlers for four years each following positive tests for AAS. In 2016, Iranian wrestler Bashir Babajanzadeh tested positive for testosterone. Zubair Dibirov, a wrestler from Azerbaijan, tested positive for the AAS stanozolol. Neither of them can return to competitions until 2020.

after ingestion. This ability to find drugs in an athlete's system after a period of many months might explain why the Russian government developed such an elaborate system to hide the abuse of AAS by its athletes.

New and improved tests make it possible to catch not only athletes competing today but also those who competed in past Olympics. One of the athletes to get caught and lose a past medal was Russian track-and-field athlete Tatyana Lebedeva. She won a gold medal for the long jump and a silver medal for the triple jump at the Beijing Olympics in 2008. But her samples from 2008 recently tested positive for AAS, and the IOC demanded that she return her Beijing medals. She has other Olympic medals and said she will not give up the two from Beijing

WHOM DO YOU BELIEVE?

When one person says AAS are dangerous and another person says they are safe, it can be hard to tell whom to believe. It helps to understand source bias. Bias occurs anytime a person's opinion is influenced by a personal view on a subject. Bias can be affected by a person's knowledge and experience. Biases are also influenced by a person's expectations and goals. For example, when a bodybuilder declares that AAS are safe, his claim is influenced by his bias. If he abuses AAS, he likely wants continued access to these substances. When doctors or scientists say AAS are unsafe, their goals are to keep people healthy and to understand the facts. When people weigh which argument to believe, they also need to look at the evidence for the person's statement. Personal experience may provide evidence, but it provides only a small amount of evidence. Experimentation and scientific studies result in a large amount of evidence. This helps researchers spot trends, such as the tendency for people who abuse AAS to develop certain illnesses and health problems.

without challenging the decision. More and more athletes may be facing the loss of their medals as the IOC develops better ways to test for AAS and PEDs.

PUBLIC HEALTH CRISIS

The abuse of AAS and other PEDs is more than a matter of cheating at a sport. It is also part of a largely unrecognized public health crisis. In 2015, the Union Cycliste Internationale (UCI), the world governing body of cycling, published a report on doping in cycling and the various factors leading to doping. The report focused on doping not only among professional athletes but also among amateur cyclists. The UCI referred to doping in amateur cycling as endemic, or common in the sport. According to the UCI's report, "It [the abuse of AAS] has been caused by a combination of ease of access to drugs via gyms and the internet, the reduction in costs for substances, a spread of knowledge in means and methods of administration, and a lack of funding for regular testing at the amateur level."[5]

Amateur athletes are not the only ones with ease of access, knowledge of what to buy, and the cash with which to buy it. Casual athletes, gym users, and high school athletes can all gain access to illegal AAS. Through steroid abuse, they may develop health problems. AAS may seem to be a quick solution, but they can turn into a long-term problem for many people who use them.

ESSENTIAL FACTS

EFFECTS ON THE BODY

- AAS are abused by people who want to build more muscle, recover from extreme muscle fatigue more quickly, enhance their physical appearance, or improve their athletic performance. Unless prescribed by a doctor, AAS are illegal in the United States because of their potential for addiction and negative health impacts.

- AAS have been linked to damage to the cardiovascular system, liver damage, and liver cancer, as well as emotional problems including suicidal depression and roid rage.

LAWS AND POLICIES

- Because AAS are against the law without a prescription in the United States, users and dealers of these drugs receive fines and prison sentences if caught. The federal penalty for the use of AAS is a fine of up to $1,000 and one year in prison for a first offense. The federal penalty for selling AAS is a fine of up to $250,000 and five years in prison for a first offense. The penalty doubles for a second offense.

- In addition, the Olympics, Major League Baseball, the National Football League, and other sports organizations have banned AAS. Athletes who test positive for AAS face suspension, fines, and loss of medals and records.

IMPACT ON SOCIETY

- Medical professionals such as Dr. Shalender Bhasin have declared the abuse of AAS in the United States to be a public health crisis because of the long-term health consequences involving heart and liver damage.

- AAS are not just a part of professional sports. Casual athletes also abuse AAS, which are available at many gyms. In two states, funds that could be spent on education are being spent on testing student athletes for AAS. Unfortunately, these tests are largely ineffective because they are not comprehensive. Students who know a test is coming can easily avoid it. Although the abuse of AAS may affect their health in later years, students see little or no immediate impact and thus are more likely to abuse these drugs.

QUOTE

"What I encounter when talking to teens is the significant pressure they feel to excel. Whether it's in sports, school, social status, or appearance, teens feel they need to be better."

—*Tyler Hamilton, anti-doping advocate*

GLOSSARY

AMPHETAMINE
A type of synthetic drug, such as methamphetamine, that is mood altering and addictive.

BLACK MARKET
A collection of buyers and sellers trading illegally.

CARDIOVASCULAR SYSTEM
The system of the body that includes the heart and blood vessels.

DOPING
Abusing performance-enhancing drugs, including anabolic-androgenic steroids.

ENDEMIC
Something that is regularly found in a given environment.

HORMONE
A regulatory substance that sparks an action, such as growth, digestion, or sexual maturation, in a tissue or organ.

LIPOPROTEIN
A protein that transports fats, or lipids, in the bloodstream.

MANIA

A mental illness that includes extreme physical activity, delusion, and excitement.

OPIUM

A type of drug that is made from the poppy plant in Europe and Asia.

PERFORMANCE-ENHANCING DRUG

A drug, such as a steroid, that helps an athlete build muscle faster, run faster, or otherwise compete at a higher level.

PLACEBO

A harmless substance that is given like a medicine to someone but that has no physical effect.

PLATELET

A disk-shaped cell found in the blood that is involved in clotting.

SEMEN

Male reproductive fluid that contains sperm.

SPERM

The male sex cell.

STIMULANT

A category of drug that affects the nervous system and increases the body's heart rate and blood pressure.

ADDITIONAL RESOURCES

SELECTED BIBLIOGRAPHY

Blickenstaff, Brian. "The New Doping Crisis Is Not a Sports Issue, It's a Public Health Issue." *Vice*. Vice, 10 Apr. 2015. Web. 30 Oct. 2017.

Grossfeld, Stan. "A Sad and Revealing Tale of Teen Steroid Use." *New York Times*. New York Times, 20 Feb. 2008. Web. 30 Oct. 2017.

Newton, David E. *Steroids and Doping in Sports: A Reference Handbook*. Santa Barbara, CA: ABC-CLIO, 2013. Print.

FURTHER READINGS

Khing, Tony. *Performance-Enhancing Drugs in Sports*. Minneapolis, MN: Abdo, 2014. Print.

Knight, Erin. *Steroids*. New York: Crabtree, 2012. Print.

ONLINE RESOURCES

Booklinks
NONFICTION NETWORK
FREE! ONLINE NONFICTION RESOURCES

To learn more about steroids, visit **abdobooklinks.com.** These links are routinely monitored and updated to provide the most current information available.

MORE INFORMATION

For more information on this subject, contact or visit the
following organizations:

NATIONAL INSTITUTE ON DRUG ABUSE

6001 Executive Boulevard
Room 5213, MSC 9561
Bethesda, MD 20892
www.drugabuse.gov

This government website provides a variety of information about steroids and
steroid abuse, including the latest studies and research.

TAYLOR HOOTON FOUNDATION

PO Box 2104
Frisco, TX 75034-9998
972-403-7300
taylorhooton.org

This nonprofit organization works to educate teens and adults about the
dangers of PEDs. The site includes information on steroids and dietary
supplements as well as stories from real teens who have been affected by
these drugs.

SOURCE NOTES

CHAPTER 1. DOPING AT THE OLYMPICS

1. Shira Springer. "In Rio, Russians Are Seen as the Villains." *Boston Globe*. Boston Globe Media, 8 Aug. 2016. Web. 10 Sept. 2017.

2. Sean Gregory. "Team USA Is About to Be Kicked Off Its Doping High Horse in Rio." *Time*. Time, 14 Aug. 2016. Web. 17 Nov. 2017.

3. Rebecca R. Ruiz and Michael Schwirtz. "Russian Insider Says State-Run Doping Fueled Olympic Gold." *New York Times*. New York Times, 12 May 2016. Web. 16 Mar. 2018.

4. Eoghan Macguire and Steve Almasy. "271 Russian Athletes Cleared for Rio Games." *CNN*. CNN, 5 Aug. 2016. Web. 26 Sept. 2017.

5. Rebecca R. Ruiz. "23 More Athletes Suspected of Doping Could Be Kept from Rio Games." *New York Times*. New York Times, 27 May 2016. Web. 30 Aug. 2017.

CHAPTER 2. STEROIDS AND TESTOSTERONE

1. Eberhard Neischlag and Susan Neischlag. "Testosterone Deficiency: A Historical Perspective." *Asian Journal of Andrology* 16.2 (2014): 161–168. Web. 28 Sept. 2017.

2. James Clear. "The Power of Placebo: What Happens When You Believe You're Taking Steroids." *Huffington Post*. Huffington Post, 31 May 2016. Web. 29 Sept. 2017.

3. "Anabolic Steroids." *ESPN*. ESPN, n.d. Web. 23 Aug. 2017.

4. Justin Peters. "The Man behind the Juice." *Slate*. Slate, 18 Feb. 2005. Web. 16 Mar. 2018.

5. Matt Chaney. "Dianabol, the First Widely Used Steroid, Turns 50 This Year." *New York Daily News*. New York Daily News, 16 June 2008. Web. 28 Sept. 2017.

CHAPTER 3. THE DOCTOR KNOWS BEST

1. "History of Testosterone." *Denver Hormone Health*. Denver Hormone Health, n.d. Web. 28 Nov. 2017.

2. Cathy Cassata. "What is Klinefelter Syndrome?" *Everyday Health*. Everyday Health, 30 Dec. 2014. Web. 2 Oct. 2017.

CHAPTER 4. SELF-PRESCRIBING

1. Julia Reed. "Marion Jones: Hail Marion." *Vogue*. Vogue, 31 Dec. 2000. Web. 16 Mar. 2018.

2. Associated Press. "Jones Stripped of Five Olympic Medals, Banned from Beijing Games." *ESPN*. ESPN, 12 Dec. 2007. Web. 3 Oct. 2017.

3. "BALCO Fast Facts." *CNN*. CNN, 27 Apr. 2017. Web. 20 Nov. 2017.

4. "Marion Jones, after Prison." *Oprah.com*. Oprah.com, 27 Oct. 2008. Web. 3 Oct. 2017.

5. Shalender Bhasin, et al. "The Effects of Supraphysiologic Doses of Testosterone on Muscle Size and Strength in Normal Men." *New England Journal of Medicine* 10.1 (1996). Web. 3 Oct. 2017.

6. Brian Orloff. "Alex Rodriguez Admits to Past Steroid Use." *People*. People, 9 Feb. 2009. Web. 16 Mar. 2018.

7. Laurie E. Scudder. "Anabolic Steroid Use in Nonathletes: Why?" *Medscape*. Medscape, 22 Aug. 2016. Web. 23 Aug. 2017.

8. Julien S. Baker, Michael Graham, and Bruce Davies. "Gym Users and Abuse of Prescription Drugs." *Journal of the Royal Society of Medicine* 99.7 (2006). Web. 3 Oct. 2017.

9. Scudder, "Anabolic Steroid Use in Nonathletes: Why?"

CHAPTER 5. ANABOLIC STEROIDS TAKE A TOLL

1. Jim Avila, Beth Tribolet, Lauren Pearle, and Scot Michels. "Girls and Steroids: Anything to Be Thin." *ABC News*. ABC News, 20 Feb. 2008. Web. 21 Sept. 2017.

2. Julian Schmidt. "Mike Matarazzo's Second Chance: Wisdom for Those Who Have a First Chance." *Flex Magazine*. Cengage Learning, 1 July 2005. Web. 5 Oct. 2017.

3. "Anabolic Steroids." *ESPN*. ESPN, n.d. Web. 23 Aug. 2017.

4. J. M. Grimes and R. H. Melloni Jr. "Prolonged Alterations in the Serotonin Neural System Following the Cessation of Adolescent Anabolic-Androgenic Steroid Exposure in Hamsters (Mesocricetus Auratus)." *Behavioral Neuroscience* 120.6 (2006): 1242–1251.

5. L. Lundholm, et al. "Anabolic-Androgenic Steroids and Violent Offending: Confounding by Polysubstance Abuse Among 10,365 General Population Men." *Addiction* 110.1 (2015): 100–108.

SOURCE NOTES CONTINUED

CHAPTER 6. STEROIDS AND THE LAW

1. Mike Riggs. "How Washington Lost the War on Muscle." *Reason*. Reason, 2017 June. Web. 16 Mar. 2018.

2. Riggs, "How Washington Lost the War on Muscle."

3. Associated Press. "BALCO Founder Conte Released from Prison." *ESPN*. ESPN, 31 Mar. 2006. Web. 6 Oct. 2017.

4. "Anabolic Steroids." *US Department of Justice*. Diversion Control Division, 2004 Mar. Web. 15 Aug. 2017.

5. "Prison Sentencing for Drugs in Texas." *Greenhouse*. Greenhouse, n.d. Web. 16 Mar. 2018.

6. "Anabolic Steroids."

7. "The Steroids Era." *ESPN*. ESPN, 5 Dec. 2012. Web. 6 Oct. 2017.

8. "The Steroids Era."

9. "The Steroids Era."

CHAPTER 7. PRESSURE TO USE

1. Rick Collins. "The 'Rising Epidemic' of Teen Steroid Abuse." *Huffington Post*. Huffington Post, 5 Jan. 2017. Web. 16 Mar. 2018.

2. Shane Stokes. "The Redemption of Tyler Hamilton." *Cycling Tips.com*. Cycling Tips.com, 29 Nov. 2016. Web. 6 Oct. 2017.

3. Samantha Olson. "Teen Steroid Use Doubled in 1 Year: What Are Parents, Coaches and the FDA Doing to Stop the Sharp Rise?" *Medical Daily*. Medical Daily, 23 July 2014. Web. 21 Sept. 2017.

4. Stokes, "The Redemption of Tyler Hamilton."

5. Jerel P. Calzo, et al. "Gender Conformity and Use of Laxatives and Muscle-Building Products in Adolescents and Young Adults." *Pediatrics* (2006). Web. 16 Mar. 2018.

6. Steven Reinberg. "Many Teen Girls Use Steroids." *ABC News*. ABC News, 23 Mar. 2017. Web. 6 Oct. 2017.

7. Jay R. Hoffman. "Do Teens Use Performance Enhancing Drugs to Emulate Their Athlete Role Models?" *ProCon.org*. ProCon.org, 15 Dec. 2008. Web. 6 Oct. 2017.

8. A. J. Gruber and H. G. Pope Jr. "Compulsive Weight Lifting and Anabolic Drug Abuse among Women Rape Victims." *Comparative Psychiatry* 40.4 (1999): 273–277. Web. 11 Jan. 2018.

9. "Women and Steroids." *Association Against Steroid Abuse*. Association Against Steroid Abuse, n.d. Web. 6 Oct. 2017.

10. Elahe Izadi. "CDC: Nearly 1 in 5 Women Have Been Raped." *Washington Post*. Washington Post, 5 Sept. 2014. Web. 22 Nov. 2017.

11. Olson, "Teen Steroid Use Doubled in 1 Year."

12. "National Study: Teens Report Higher Use of Performance Enhancing Substances." *PR Newswire*. PR Newswire, 23 July 2014. Web. 16 Mar. 2018.

13. Alexandra Pannoni. "Doping Rises Among High Schoolers, but Few Districts Test." *US News and World Report*. US News and World Report, 11 Aug. 2014. Web. 6 Oct. 2017.

14. "The Two States Testing HS Athletes for Steroids Turn Up Few Positives." *USA Today*. USA Today, 16 Sept. 2016. Web. 6 Oct. 2017.

15. "Bigorexia: Young Men, Body Image, and Steroids." *ABC.net.au*. ABC.net.au, 10 Mar. 2014. Web. 5 Oct. 2017.

CHAPTER 8. ADDICTION AND WITHDRAWAL

1. Ruth I. Wood. "Anabolic-Androgenic Steroid Dependence? Insights from Animals and Humans." *Frontiers in Neuroendocrinology* 29.4 (2008): 490–506. Web. 23 Nov. 2017.

2. Wood, "Anabolic-Androgenic Steroid Dependence?"

3. "NCAA National Study of Substance Use Habits of College Student Athletes." *NCAA*. NCAA, July 2014. Web. 16 Mar. 2018.

4. Tiffany Esmat. "Measuring and Evaluating Body Composition." *American College of Sports Medicine*. American College of Sports Medicine, 7 Oct. 2016. Web. 16 Mar. 2018.

5. Ginger Gorman. "The Deadly Crusade to Get Ripped." *News.com.au*. News.com.au, n.d. Web. 23 Nov. 2017.

6. Stan Grossfeld. "A Sad and Revealing Tale of Teen Steroid Use." *New York Times*. New York Times, 20 Feb. 2008. Web. 5 Oct. 2017.

CHAPTER 9. THE FIGHT CONTINUES

1. "Well-Known Gym Caught in Multi-State Steroid Ring Sting." *CBS*. CBS, 22 Feb. 2017. Web. 24 Nov. 2017.

2. Anna Medaris Miller. "Before You Try Steroids to Build Muscle, Read This." *US News and World Report*. US News and World Report 21 Apr. 2016. Web. 24 Nov. 2017.

3. Miller, "Before You Try Steroids to Build Muscle, Read This."

4. Associated Press. "Texas Lawmakers Prepared to Pull Funding for $10 Million Steroid Testing System for High School Athletes." *New York Daily News*. New York Daily News, 23 Mar. 2015. Web. 7 Oct. 2017.

5. Brian Blickenstaff. "The New Doping Crisis Is Not a Sports Issue, It's a Public Health Issue." *Vice Sports*. Vice Sports, 10 Apr. 2015. Web. 7 Oct. 2017.

INDEX

ABOUT THE AUTHOR

Sue Bradford Edwards is a Missouri nonfiction author who writes about health, science, history, and race. She has written more than 12 books for Abdo Publishing, including *The Dakota Access Pipeline*, *The Zika Virus*, *Women in Science*, and *Hidden Human Computers*.